INDELICATE ANGELS

INDELICATE ANGELS

Ismael García Santillanes

Rainshadow Editions
The Black Rock Press
University of Nevada, Reno
2014

ISBN 978-1-891033-66-7
Library of Congress Control Number: 2014936528
Printed in the United States of America

The Black Rock Press
University of Nevada, Reno
Reno, NV 89557-0224
www.blackrockpress.org

Cover artwork by the author

CONTENTS

PART III: MOTHER'S BOOK OF THE DEAR

PART IV: SCREAMING IN THE BUGHOUSE

ACKNOWLEDGEMENTS

Some of the poems in this book appeared in the following journals:

Bristlecone (Carson City, Nevada)
Collages & Bricolages (Clarion, Pennsylvania)
Goatfoot Press (Salem, Oregon)
Interim (Las Vegas, Nevada)
Pegasus (Boulder City, Nevada)
Prison Life Magazine (New York, New York)
Razor Wire (Carson City, Nevada)
Sierra Nevada College Review (Incline Village, Nevada)
Talking River Review (Lewiston, Idaho)
Weber Studies (Ogden, Utah)

"Jimmy Took Too Long To Die" was included in the anthology *New Poets of the American West* (2010 Many Voices Press, Flathead Valley Community College, Kalispell, Montana)

The author's work on this book was supported in part by a 2008 Literary Fellowship/Grant from the Sierra Arts Foundation of Reno, Nevada

I

PICKING GRAPES

Love is Always Written on the Water of Our Bodies

Unless I close my eyes and gently
press the hollow to my throat
to feel the ocean of my body pulse
against my fingertips,
I cannot see you laugh
that summer night you pranced
on lithe legs stemmed
from the fray of jean cutoffs
over the water banked
on the koi pond at Nacho's ranch.

My hands were runes carved
on the mystery of your body,
a moon moist book whose pages
I turned to translate
with a Mexican tongue
into the myth you became
a wild white witch who tore
my back as we pitched on the mud.

Unless I conjure
the quiet earth of my heart,
I cannot sustain your breath
laced in my hair as we broke
the eucharist of our bodies,
then drew down
the moon's white gauze
to wash the parchment
of blood and seed
into the cool koi pond.

i love you like a peasant

—mxolisi nyezwa

i cannot pretend to love you
white, beautiful woman.

i am not a rose from your garden
whose petals you may eat.

february's crystal sky
is flush of its magnificence,
but like it, i will not forget
when the clouds have blown
and the frost has veined...

what the kiss meant,
how quiet the world became,
so hush i heard nevada's lizards
wosling over sand.

A Peasant's Prayer

Over the Washoe basin,   a rain cloud stretches:

    a tympanic membrane
    pressed against the small backs of human voices...

A wisp of prayer   escapes my lips:

    against the goatskin cloud
    it sibilates...

Nimbostratus ions   synapse:

    the cloud's nerves fracture,
    prayer cracks throughout the sky...

To fall, my love,   so far away.

For Whom I Fall

We sat, held, talked
and kissed as if our lips
      had fallen upon
a first memory.

We did not hold back,
save poems
      for what of poetry
when tongues can read

mouths' braille.

Adrift On A Blue Love Seat

On the blue, uncomfortable love seat,
the one on which, if we lean too long
to one side, our legs fall asleep,

so we have to stand up often
to shake out the needles and pins,
the one on which I seem to drift

so far you think you've lost me.
Well, let me tell you, missy,
when my eyes are two stars set

in some distant galaxy
of russet clay and green rivers,
it's quite all right for you to visit,

to mess up my hair, there
on that blue, uncomfortable love seat
on which I lean to my imaginings.

Moose Have Lips

I wonder who you are,
woman who sleeps on her back like a cub,
awakes at midnight to explain:

> The exact moment something happens,
> it's inevitable.

Then prods me to the den
to bare our bodies
as the Public Television Station
transmits a nature segment:

horrified teenage moose,
beautiful boy, broken ballerino,
ribs ripped open by fangs of bear.
He dies: incredulous, flaccid brown eyes;
moose lips bloom black rose petals.

On the couch, soft, sinuous feet
push at my hip; you feign a swoon,
mimic lips of that fallen ruminant.

Your wisdom:

> Teenage moose status
> is determined by the lack of phallic distraction
> while trying to get away.

We cuddle, suckle on each other's tongues,
two starving children waiting for the sun.

The Slap

I was never convinced
you would not slap me,
having as a boy
seen it done to a man
so sure of love
as grease and oil pans,
who found counsel
away from crowds
in the familiar smells
of his garage:

>   tools in cardboard boxes
>   bargained for at swap meets,
>   a bowl-shape dinted hub cap
>   used to soak parts
>   in WD-40,
>   then wrung dry
>   with an old shirt,
>   sturdy blue plastic
>   Model Dairy milk crate
>   used as a foot stool
>   to help lean against
>   musky army blanket draped
>   over the fender beneath the hood
>   of his '75 Valiant,
>   there to fondle the phantom
>   of her fierce hand
>   lay waste
>   against his skin ablaze...

Learning back then
this is what is meant of men,
to take the anger of a woman
to torque the certainty of bolts,
wished it all upon myself,
was left behind the deafening hollow.

Mourning The Death Of Coffee Cups

You held a fragment,
ceramic shard,
as you would
a child's broken arm.

"A stupid accident," you stabbed,
then the silent stare that pled,
"Come rescue me."

But I was not prepared
to cuddle the casualty
of accusations
kindled in the palms
of an empty pillow.

"A stupid accident,"
I tried the words for truth,

       then walked away.

Moth Water Walk

Next to the bench on the dock,
a photo-sensitive switch
trips the lamppost on.
The lamp light buzz,
luminous muezzin in a minaret,
calls night moths to prayer.

My eyeballs are the spots
on the back of a moth's wings.
Wherever it goes,
I see everything it flies from:

> a hungry bird;
> a child's clumsy hand;
> a warm, brick wall;
> your photograph
> in the sweaty palm of a lonely man.

Perhaps my body
is the spot on the back of a moth,
the ferry
fluttering its paddles across sound...

I see everything it flies from.

If Naomi Were My Lover

I promise
not to last forever,

to leave
only the impression

of my body,
the scent

of ravenous words
tongued against teeth,

then draw back
into my own

to measure
the impermanence

I am.

It Started When I Was Eight

I hid under a rack
of women's lingerie,
eating Mexican candy,
so sweet and so bitter.

That jungle
of silkworm lace
was cool shade
for a little boy
with tired feet.

I looked up
through a gown
of delicate weave,
hallucinated
a pretty face,
breasts brushed
against glass silk,
bent wrists,
pale hands,
tiny belly button,
long legs
in a Hollywood movie.

Her genitals
I imagined
a mannequin,
a Barbie Doll.

At eight
I had not yet
conceived
of peach fuzz
and nectar.

Indelicate Angels

Swan diving
off abandoned railroad tracks
sutured over red rust river
like an open wound.

I followed the flight
of skinny dipping screams
streamed down
dirty water discourse.

We bathed
in that desert vein,
a pair of wingless
indelicate angels.

Our bodies
littered the bank
like two pieces
of pallid driftwood.

We rolled
in red clay,
cut our backs
on green bottle shards.

Our faces
masked in mud
provided
the answer to love:

oxidize wise water
with laughter,
and let
the desert bleed.

Full Moon Scripture

> Touch me,
> remind me who I am.
> —Stanley Kunitz

Beneath the full, moth-white moon
still rising to skim across the koi pond,

in the small clearing within the cattail reed,
our indelicate bodies bowed the mud bank.

On the wet silt and clay, we were
the hieroglyphs of laughter and love,

each graceless line of us read
in the honey thick of whispered asylums,

a moth-white moon skimming across
our bodies' scripture of blood and seed.

Looking For A Place To Park

Pursing our lips
to green glassy necks
of St. Pauli Girls.
The Rolling Stones
fondled Angie on the radio.
You were the girl
who swore off men
in consummate suffering
with werewolves.

Cruising
the night-drenched back roads,
the Buick's sunroof
was a thin-veiled hymen
you popped
by standing on the seat.
Screeching at the stars
with your large nipples,
you were the witch
down Painted Canyon Road.

So who was I to argue
when you wanted someone
not entirely yours.

Picking Grapes

I

The vines in the vineyard
grow outward,
a puritanical hoop skirt
hiding its fruit...

Once exposed
I could tell
by the tautness of skin
how easily it would bust open,
ripe enough to eat...

At thirteen,
I was always hungry.

II

Alex knew
why some women's pelvic bones
jutted out more than others:

Those whose hips grow wide
are meant to have children
saddled on the small of waist,
one on each side...
I thought about Juanita,
balanced a box
of black grapes on my shoulder,
sank through the sand
like a monster.

III

I knew why Tammy ran out screaming,
her white pants
bleeding where she sat.

I had seen the instructions,
tossed in the bathroom's paper basket,
diagrammed to show my sisters
how to place one leg
on the toilet seat cover,
then insert...

gently ...

I snipped off a bundle
of seedless pearlet,
and in that moment understood
why women
make such a fuss
about the toilet seat,
it being a part of their ceremony.

IV

Pia washed it clean
before she peeled back
skin on a fat purple grape,
exposed purple veins,
lapped up the juice
running down
the length of her fingers,
then bit it in half...

"So I won't,"
she said,
"swallow the seed."

V

Sugar levels rise at night,
siphoned through vines
from Earth's old belly...

Lynette stood still
as she invited me
to breathe with our hands ...

We could have been the first
to feel so much pain
in so tender exchange.

VI

What's left behind
becomes too ripe,
but makes excellent fruit
for the brewing of wine ...

Women intoxicate me ...

How during mass
they would poise rosaries
next to their lips,
shawls draped over heads,
the image of the Virgin Herself

perfumed in Chanel #5
or Midnight Passion ...

In the name of the Sun,
the Earth,
and Their Fruit
I would pray ...

But at thirteen,
I was always hungry.

En Tijuana

Even the prostitutes are kind;
a hard kindness
      rakes in their eyes
      to humble my head;
this well groomed *pocho* head;
these clandestine threads
layered for aesthetics; antithesis
to *pesadilla de pobresa.*

Pero aquí estoy; here I am
with sterile hands; my broken
tongue; *esta lengua*
que no habla revolución;
to whom Quetzalcoatl means
the albino snake slithered
on the muscles
of Salma Hayek's ass.

Yes, *mis prostitutes de pobresa,*
I am the endemic American *pocho;*
poached; only half cooked.

*pocho: Chicano who speaks broken Spanish and lacks in Mexican culture

The Buddha Has A Brittle Blue Head

The summer-blistered air was full of pain.
For seven weeks the bastard sun
plagued the linseed sky.
Then fell the hot rain.
Droplets the size of thumbs
exploded on the pond's taut skin.

On a tractor tire inner tube
meant for bodies who love like slugs,
I put to lip a lukewarm demijohn
to toast the sting of lust,
then paddled out to the middle of the pond.

From the reeds along the bank,
I heard the chirps of warbles,
hidden from the beak of the sun,
bickering like intellectuals
about the compassion of clouds
and the coolness of mud.
But I was there to starve my soul
of a girl who stole this Promethean's furnace.

Now there's no accounting
for the way women move, except to say
they learn at a very young age.
So knowing that, and being the
Bodhisattva beatnik with a sense of mist,
I prayed to Buddha between the sips
of that beautiful drunk delirious buoyancy:

Dear, dear Buddha
With the brittle blue head,
Please allow me to forget...

How Juanita thrust back knees, straight legs locked,
stood akimbo, pelvic bone thrust,
lust layered on the pout of her lips,
the swell of her hair, the scent of her sweat,
as her buttocks culminated for all men
in episodes of deep breathing exercises...

Brother, I tell you, she had a following.

When Mr. Mebark's Daughter Dances

The glassing woo of rosary beads
   nor a fist of prayers
         through the gut can save me...

The flash stop coruscant bark
   of black lit white spine
         undulated down

         to a round, resonant ass...

You must know what you do to me...

Gyrating tight, black latex pants,
   like a God's wife
         gone Egyptian whore:

         eyes scored black of ash,
         hands of henna thick of men,
         hips that coil and pitch,

         scent of oil, beads of sweat,
         kisses tether from breasts
         to explode upon my body's sand...

I am left a shambled man.

Promethean Godde

for rosslynn

Flower-printed miniskirt
is gauze around
California baby doll,

buttocks swaddled
in a swath of silk
tug with every step,

arms syncopate
away the glassy legs
of champagne bottles,

hips flare then give
to the small
of waist,

a smile warns:
Soy chula, but difficult
to get along with.

To The Girl With A Teardrop Tattoo

Some deep dug thing stirs in this man
before a blue teardrop tattoo
on the cheek of a girl with cinnamon skin,

some animal thing so deep awakened,
sharp teeth shot spine down,
makes me step all monosyllabic,

so ancient a thing stirs at the scent
of brown sugar skin,
long unkempt sienna hair,

says you are gypsy and still dancing,
that faded blue teardrop tack,
hard life stigma,

makes this man full of want
and all at once cautious,
a deep dug thing stirs in the gut,

so deep I think it's primitive,
like some fertility ritual
done in blood on cave walls,

that I, so struck, forget how
to rid my soul of lust so raw
it sorts this man of words.

Elpidia Carrillo

—as she appeared in Predator,
dreamt of her.

Clung to your brown
stone-washed nipples,
dirty white BVD,
chaffed by the pricks
of a flesh-starved jungle
you swore swallowed
a band of guerrilleros
whose names you bore
from it cool black core.

We shred off clothes,
your small breasts,
brown loaves for a Mayan god,
the portable banged out
the closest to a love song
by Sublime

> If it wasn't for date rape,
> I'd never get laid...

But we were too intense for that
cliché Seattle shit
as we crumpled to the ground...
Your thin lips were hunger for words,
my poems, drove mad
your refugee hands,
wound around the wound of me,
then scorched against

the fuzz of your belly,
raw cock ground
'til drained
our bones of breath.

Chin Kyong Cha On Her Virgin Cloth

So lightly on the iridescent silkworm lace
the apple blossoms were embroidered,
wisped beneath your smoothing hand.

The air, lit of jasmine-scented paraffin,
flamed its slanted eyes.

Gentled to the floor, your robe was a cloud
another virgin could have toed.

Your body, lithe as a white ceramic teapot neck,
laid upon the virgin's cloth with love
so lightly parted. The apple blossoms blushed.

Loving Chin Kyong Cha

We were the vigorous muscles
on the sweaty backs
of laboring oxen
our hands
four thick
oxen tongues
lapping ourselves
like newborn calves
my penis a piece
of purple-tipped dough
her clitoris
exhausted farmer
hunched over
a single furrow
cleared for farming
our bodies clinging
flesh liquid
pouring ourselves
into ourselves
till morning came
all over the rice fields
to find us in bed
a puddle
of gasping hearts.

Chin Kyong Cha's Nocturnal

As you slept,
I held you
like a violin,
your head
snugly tucked
below my chin,
my left hand
felt way down
your fretless arm,
gently fingered
tendon chords,
subdermal,
imperceptible,
my right
horsehair fingers
pizzicato plucked
the buttons
from your night shirt,
sul ponticello
played the bow
close to the bridge,
col legno
with the wooden part,
you woke up
to a full standing orchestra,
before *tremolo*
and the loss
of consciousness again.

Chin Kyong Cha Loved To Explain

Standing nude at the window
where rice paddies deflected
sunshine to her form...

> The trill birds make
> sounds terrible to them
> so they do it in the morning
> to annoy us, when in fact
> we fall in love...

But when she said it in Korean,
it sounded
like a poorly tuned guitar.

Chin Kyong Cha Taught Me How To Eat With Chopsticks

Eating burritos
with chopsticks,
she said,

> *as if an old man*
> *is crossing his legs.*

Said women created
delicate utensils
to make men, while they eat,
seem effeminate,
then tore through
the hot tortilla,

> *as if an old man*
> *is taking a step.*

She picked up
a piece from her plate
to her mouth,

> *as if an old man*
> *is scooping up grandchildren.*

Making Emma Madly Scream

for Gailmarie's Emma
from Ismael's werewolf

I

Emma,
I don't know
what the desert wants of me.

Sometimes so desperately
I dream of riding
on a red ant
over the amber fossil
of your clit.

A vicious anthropologist
powders it
for fingerprints.

II

Peeling an orange,
I expected your sleepy body
to be one of the slices.

I kissed the part
I thought should be
the nape,
from which dreams, nested,
are summoned.

Your navel
   is the seed
      for a voluminous tree.

III

I am not one
to mask
immense laughter.

But like you (perhaps like you)...

   I scrap...

even with those I love.

Queen of Otters

What is it you feed
        your little horribles
whose sleek black bodies
        like animated
                grande soirée gloves
        treat at your feet

before they rift
        through water warped

along the river bank?

        Is this what becomes
        of a woman wilderness aged?

When the moon shadows are long,
        you stream
                for a dip in the nude,

are the otters allowed
        to play with your thighs,
                their torsos

thick as a man's arms?

        Sweet queen, spinster,
        lover of teeth and fur,

why feed them so much fruit?

On The Ocean Of A Barefooted Gypsy

The morning's pungent scent
    of your sex made sweet
        all a man could dream of doing

as I contemplated daybreak tangled
    on the glistening tuft and how
        a woman knew by touch to shush

the thinning birr that wears a man...
    Turkish eyes that swayed like scythes,
        the tortured thicket of obsidian hair

that swelled and crashed on the white shore
    of an undulating spine as my belly
        pitched in that Black Sea squall

pulsing through the wrung-wet thighs
    of Istanbul...From my nipples
        your Romany-pidgin tongue diffused

over my body's Mexican onion skin
    like a hennaed treatise on what
        a woman can do to a man

or the scrying of man's scars
    as jaws fanged and hairy legs arched
        on the ocean on a woman's humped back

who came in a timbre so low it rolled
    through my spine, the earth, aquifers,
        through the bodies of whales,

then spilled from the hull of your flesh,
   a soft stem, and the matted hair of the abdomen
      were serifs in that old world dialect

of women who dance in bare feet.

How To Kiss A Werewolf

Do not kiss me as an act of kindness.

Conjure my tongue to slant with depravation,
    let the weight of sin drip
           to the pit of my stomach...

Make it feel nasty.

Gothic Girl Walking On The Sidewalk: First Sighting

A prayer strangely come,
consequences of a man not thought out;
a prayer, fallacy of human doubt,
she come:

> black boot alloy
> Elizabethan hobnail and stiletto;
> pants, the fundament
> to affect mental damage;
> bodice embroidered of black thorns;
> onyx sharp as a cock's talons,
> butchered hair, eyes, mouth...
> as if dignity was gothic sumi
> on bleached rice paper...

A prayer strangely come,
anathema to the self-inflicted cognates,
the cultural inbreeding of the religious wrong...

I knew right then, this penitent,
this bastard of original sin

is prone to mental damage.

Gothic Girl-Watching At The Teahouse

I: (writing poems)

I whisper   each caesura:

affection in those who sense bodiless virtues,
the analgesic sip of black tea,
or fall for the shrill dark stare of gothic girls.

II: (anima archetype)

She steams her hand   over a teacup:

mullein clips and chamomile.
Sat, her body coils
into wrought-ironed Cyrillic runes:

       dementia praecox,
          vampire,
        pathos,
       things that stop breathing an eternity...

I know those synodical Jungian scapes,
those caesuras   whispered like prayer, gone...

would be too much for any young man.

III: (animus archetype)

Steam-clung bergamot, my tea
is a galaxy of swirling bodhisattvas,
its perfume, a soporific.
The world around the cup disintegrates,
to the serried whir of om I go
long enough to sense my own divinity:

> a soothing psychosis
>   werewolf,
>   a quiet ecstasy,
>   things that stop breathing an eternity...

But those Jungian scapes
that put aside   the curse of flesh

are nothing but play for a man my age.

IV: (on forever)

My lips purse   the teacup rim

to cool the swirl of bodhisattvas;
steam nostrils to my head...
It forgives:

> like blood from the wrist,
>   a mother at the cross
>   of a stupid child,
>   things that cannot stop eternity...

She stares back and I   hold still.

The Gothic Girl Asked How A Werewolf Is Conceived

It is not aroused through prayer
nor the scent of wiccan paraffin,
but a bodhisattva with a chemistry set...

a dram of loneliness,
a dram of love,
a cauldron's brew
of the unsayable said,
the five fold kiss,
and a wish to live...

Suddenly, the way all women come to know,
a mild anxiety unfolds.

Breakfast With The Gothic Girl

I don't mind your feet on the breakfast table:

toenails painted black,
        waned ankles,
        long tibias,
        the inner thigh tattoo of a crucifix...

I know where they cede,
how perfectly shaved you are,
how willing to show me your scars.

You slip a vampire white finger
into a cup of cold black coffee, to say...

        the crucifixion
        was didactics on gothic piercings...
        theophanic impotence
        of a deadbeat father...
        how every daughter worships

        like Magdalene...

You let the word hang with your eyes...

I wait for you to stir back from that apprehension,
for any moment, your gothic black hell to seize me...

to make love while you think of those you hate.

The Gothic Girl Sleeps In The Afternoon

O nude, tenuous vampire,
it is not so much for this artist
the sumi sketches I make of you,

nor the Cyrillic precept tattooed
on your skin
like scorn,

but the unpretentious way
you lie so
obscenely beautiful...

A younger man would reach for you.

The Gothic Girl In Late From A Yosano Akiko Reading

Because I know a man is useless
in the midst of your undressing,
I atone my heartbeat
to wait,

for you to walk in,
breath still fresh of cherry blossoms,
Akiko's tankas fluttering
around your tongue like razor blades.

Morning Prayer Over The Body Of The Gothic Girl

Let this prayer   spill forever from my heart,

the creed of love be drawn on goth-white skin
in the numinous ink of dawn,

like scars of light across her body,
the stark white rune of ridicule,

but o, my heart   how worn of love.

Gothic Girl At A Conservative Social Gathering

Slant vampire, punk white skin,
the anti-paradigm to pretense:

> the samurai inside you,
> still tattered from the last war,
> hand gentle silk upon the sword...

You move among them,
postulants to precepts:

> men steal glances over glasses of wine,
> nourish middle-aged proclivities...

> women, woven in the womb
> to measure man's malfeasance,
> wonder who the fuck invited you.

Watching The Gothic Girl Eat A Peach

There is no beautiful word   to describe you:

      the vituperations that pulse
      just below Cyrillic white skin...

No feral pretense   as fingers thin

      around the peach like razor scars.

No hubris   as you flesh teeth:

      the bite, the suckling down
      the arm to the breakfast table.

There is no beautiful word   to dissuade

      that I shall be to you as vulgar...

But what a lovely distraction.

Tacitly

and you give yourself away
—U2

your eyes unravel the morning light
but there is no man to gather you,
no one to love you back to sleep
to keep your hands from blowing away
like wind white dandelion seed.

A Woman Sound

—for Lynn

I want to hear
the beautiful sound
a woman makes
the sound that makes
a woman rise
as the day rises
then falls
her belly falls
despite the day
having risen
having fallen
having wanted to hear
the beautiful woman sound.

How A Woman Quiets A Man

1.

it started with a tree
someone thought was beautiful,

a woman's hand, henna-ed
hemmed beneath a leaf,

a stem snapped silence:
the fruit full of seed...

2.

the pomegranates you picked,
sun brazed, dead leafed,
ignite their cool seed in our mouths.

3.

he awed at the woman's ability for language:

not pretty thing: *meadow saffron*
not legged bird: *sacred ibis*

not touch, but moisture
in a kiss is collateral detriment.

4.

our mouths dyed alizarin crimson,
the acerbic rind tossed,

your kiss moist on a stem of silence,

your hand hemmed
to the leaf, my heart.

Fall Hush

The February pogonip is hush,
a fog in which my heart like smoke unfolds,
and I recall a time before your kiss—
as if the colophon of me were blank
and all the possibilities for love
were new. Yet still, despite the ache, I fall

without another heart to break my fall—
no woman's fingertip to sweetly hush
the poetry I whisper for her love.
So many years since anyone unfolds
the leaves that are my lungs, the blades gone blank.
The want has worn away that final kiss

and lust must lure from memory the kiss
that lured my heart to trust I'd never fall,
the kiss that made, like pogonip, go blank
the colophon, the blades of lungs, go hush
their poetry—so hush, the heart unfolds
to move within the quietness of love

as once I moved, a stupid man in love.
Yet here I am, afraid to write your kiss
can go to hell, that when the fog unfolds
and memory comes back, I will not fall—
afraid I can't coerce the heart be hush
when every time I write a line in blank

or measured verse, my heart, itself as blank
as any page that scripts itself of love,
can hear my lungs recite within the hush
caesuras of its beats the end-stopped kiss.
So, damned by any means, I choose to fall—
to cede my heart as memory unfolds

the writing in my lungs and so unfolds
that time before your mouth wooed blank
this poet's tongue. To revel in the fall,
I choose my lungs to read aloud of love,
to crave a woman's fingertips and kiss,
to set ablaze the heart—forget the hush...

The February fog unfolds like love
its lungs gone blank, so I recount the kiss—
then both, who know of solitude, fall hush.

Looking At Szymborska's Photograph

If my hands are grafted to your wrists—
for whatever reason—it doesn't matter—
and as you go about your day,
I feel the things you touch,
will that cigarette I see
on the cover photo of your book
be the first thing you reach for?
It will feel foreign to me, the filter turn
hot as smoke drags into your mouth.

Then what—the coffee cup?
So unnatural the fulcrum of a cup,
apparent how when hung on a hook
or dangled from the distal phalanx of the index,
it tilts and empties—like a good life.

Resting on the saucer,
the spoon tells me you take sugar—
a commodity I always link to war.
And even without the familiar weight of it,
the blind metal says the spoon is yours.

What of other things quotidian? I assume
you live as others do. The books behind you
have been read, I'm sure. The small, framed mirror
on the shelf, I take, is just a little place
to remind your face belongs to you.

But if you find at any time my hands
are slow to know how words are wrung,
just give them someone to love,
and right before they come undone like galaxies,
read the palms, and there you will find
lines agreeable to both of us.

A Whale's Letter Of Love

I.
Through the ocean   from a great distance,

      a whale feels
      a love song pulse against its body...

It rolls and tumbles like a child.

II.
I prefer   the harsh winter

      sharp inside the lung,
      the air's frozen acrimony

      so heavy hung,
      I feel a song pulse

the low throb   of another heart.

III.
Perhaps this is not meant   for a letter

      but that I should throw these words
      into the ocean

      for a species with a bigger heart...

But how,   my love,

      will you hear my song

among so many whales.

Growing Tomatoes With Marcy White

I cannot help you in the garden today,
not for another nine years.
That's nine seasons of pulling weeds,
of turning your back on the sun to face the earth.

Listen. Lower yourself with indiscretion.
Let the soil sample your thighs.
Whisper into the seed your secrets.
Sow them into the earth (this
is called the lighting death).
Now work the earth.

Seedlings will stalk up the sun.
Tomatoes will hang from the wire trellis
like angry testicles plump with seed.

The first one you pluck, share with the earth.
Cast your circle. Draw down the sun.
Tear the red fruit open on a flat rock.
Scry it for love.

The rest seal in boiling Kern jars.
Kiss them to sleep in a dark, cool place.

In nine years,
if they say it's okay for me to leave,
your tomatoes will awaken to the mouth of a hungry man.

II

MOTHER'S BOOK OF THE DEAD

What The Weeds In A Cotton Field Taught Me

for my flesh and blood

Down the sun on the Coachella Valley presses
on my forty-six year old mother and my
fourteen year old labor-wracked back,

hired by the Marshburn Bros. to weed their fields,
through two layers of brown cotton Jersey gloves,
my boy soft hands cultivate a small town of blisters.

I lift hoe blade only enough to graze
over clods of dried dirt, then sharp down
to fell any trying green plant not cotton.

I hate this work: this unforgiving damnation.
It reminds me how poor we are, and how poor people
have to sell their muscle at minimum wage.

But I keep going because my mother keeps going,
her field worker body hunched over each row
as if she were reading a prayer. I try

to read the same prayer, but my heart
is in contradiction to this life. I don't
want to live in a skin of sweat and dirt.

Yet, twenty-five years later, I will know
how a son's love for his mother can assuage
any shame for how hard we worked enough

to write it down for the whole damned world to weigh.

The Pope Of Chickens

They feed on seed aspersed from her fist,
beaks full of sin,
feet, yellow furrowed rinds,
draw   step
   draw   step
in the shadow of my mother's dress.

The Skirt Of Mother's Knife

Before my mother took the knife, to cut
a tender scion from the stalk, she'd shut
her eyes to sense the voice of chlorophyll

imbue her mind, the pith of bliss and will,
the vining tendrils of her love, to still
the leafless stem. She'd say, her voice like thread,

Así nos toma dios con tanta sed.
But I could never tell that what she said
was said to me or to the plants who kept

their stories to themselves. And so I stepped
along, an acolyte who gladly swept
his twiggy shadow next to mother's skirt.

The way she held the knife was to assert
a knowing root, and with a pinch of dirt,
she'd bless the blade. The wound was clean and quick,

then poulticed with organic resin, thick
of kitchen-whispered prayers meant to wick
away *la maldición.* I had no doubt.

I'd seen my thorny siblings take. Throughout
the garden rose the grafted stems, devout
to mother's touch as if to destiny.

She'd wisp, "Así te trajo dios a mí,"
then graft the shoot to cleft. But in that wee
incredible existence children know,

I only understood that even though
I'd come to know the cut that lets me go,
that I'd be grafted to another life
to dance around the skirt of mother's knife.

In Mother's Kitchen

I see your eyes
take sadness by the chicken neck
to chop its head off

sharpen my eyes
on your words
sitting at the table

sipping on peppermint
like a snake being milked
for venom

your stories make
the chambers to my heart
flap like angry mouths

tell me twice how nice it was
to splash his face
with hot coffee

how he sliced your arm
with his blade
then beat you with his fists

as you tried desperately
to save the child
kicking back at him

through the skin
of your belly
left you for dead

his handprints wrapped
around your neck
but the child's heart

inside you kept you alive
even when yours had stopped
and how that is why

you have always called
my brother
mi vida.

The Quiet Tongue

The cow tongue
   mother flopped
      on the cutting board

   said nothing

of the first bull
   that mounted
      her thick back

   who broke

her breath
   like bread
      a eucharist

and when the cleaver
   swished through
      like a wet whisper

   only I winced.

Genealogy Of Apprehension

(February. Midnight. Everyone is asleep.)

A disquieting stillness awakens me,
whispering undertones,
an apprehension sewn into spine,

genetic quilting of character,
frayed fibers of predisposition
a son begins to cultivate

while still in the womb,
stone washed in amnion dye,
then nurtured while mother unearthed

bulbs and taproots chopped up
along with cow tongue to stew
in black cast iron pot

all without saying a single word,
with only the slightest trace of anxiety,
like the verse of domesticity,

written in the lines of her face,
the sense of waking up to quiet things
sipped from mother's cow tongue soup.

At The Nursing Home

—from a dream

I touch your face,
afraid your skin will peel away
at the warmth of my hand.

The nurse apologizes
for the way you wear your dress,
but you insisted on doing it yourself.

Your lipstick bleeds
at the corners of your mouth.

What's left of your hair
slept flat
for too long on one side.

Dear flesh,
dear mother,
you smell disinfected
for my visit.

You still go through
a list of sons' names
before you get to mine.

When I was a kid,
I used to think that was funny.

And you would say,
"Someday you'll be old."

An attendant
offers to push you outside,
"To get," he says, "a little sun..."
When I was twelve
you took me to work
picking grapes
in the Coachella Valley.
I hid from the blaring sun
beneath the vines...

I wheel you outside anyway.

The cobblestone is smooth;
the wheelchair gives only a little.

A group of abandoned eyes
adopt me as their son.

They touch my sides
as I stroll by
as if touching their Savior's robe.

I feel drained.

I wish to dismiss their connection to me.
I wish to die without their understanding.

Without their hunger.

Yet I know someday
I too will sit
beneath the sun,
beneath the earth...

I too will hunger for a son
to visit.

Dear Intrusive Death

Leave my mother alone.

She is waned of love:

>   her daughters and sons
>   took it all.

We left only
prescription pills,
a searching face bowled
in a pair of spotted hands.

We have broken her water too often.

Take instead a woman
who has never broken water:

>   she will be more filled with love...

even for a son-of-a-bitch like you.

Mother's Book Of The Dead

Mother, when you die, you will attack giant windmills with a rolling pin, feed soft figs to a choir of toothless women, show off my graduation picture to every other mother there in the Great Void. However, conversations with the dead will bore you...

In showing off my graduation picture, you will remember you never did get me to climb off the roof. You will reincarnate just to try one last time to cajole me down into your harsh hush. You will succeed only when you allow me to wield the rolling pin to strike down the small birds that eat the ripe figs with such rapture...

But the giant windmills, mother, how am I to defend your corpse while you are gone?

for us the war is gone

no longer will i wage war on the windmills, mother.
your corpse is of no interest to them,
my stance over your body of no use.
the wooden sword i used as a child to fight them off
now makes better pyre wood...

those *mendigo* birds that used to swoop
down on the figs are laughing at me...

they know i once flew.
my wings were your songs cooking breakfast,
my beak swooped down to spoon
your mexican soup.

while you were snowed by hospice drugs
that make a body unfist the last of living,
the sound of your voice void of its music

broke my rhythm. i fell.
the windmills swarmed to pin me down,
to pluck the last of your songs from my scapulas...

without your breath in this world,
i try but can't make my body remember
how it felt to fly,
so i lower my head

and walk.

Until The Color Is Gone

I cannot hold
my mother's wrinkled hands
while she
grows
old

nor look into
her eyes
discolored
slowly
by the pain

of having cried
through
nights
loveless
alone

for having gone
to church
to witness
other
women

with
my father
leading
them
in choir

every
rosary bead
a drop
of cyanide
in her heart

I remember
how
she cried
into
my arms

confessed
she felt
my father
drift
away

if ever
she felt empty
while praying
to
her god

it was then
when she
felt worn
and
old.

For Grandmother The Earth Held No More Secrets

Only the earth
was calloused enough
to consume her lust,

too heavy
for her sons,

perhaps her daughters,
if each breathe
and push   and push
each their own flesh,

may learn to cradle
her lust
in their arms, breasts,

their mouths
may sing their hands
into the old she was,

into the bent earth
she learned to consume.

In A Chilton Manual For A Chevrolet Truck

Unable to read English, your finger
would trace diagrams
to see how things were put together:

> Zerk fittings on ball joints;
> the dance between rack and pinion;
> pistons; valves; how plugs sparked
> from the electrical pulse of a distributor cap;
> the oil's course from pan, up
> trickled into the engine block
> to keep the valves cool and flapping.

Mexican words for human parts
would describe the things you pointed at
page after page, beneath the precision
of your Chevrolet truck, jacked and blocked
to accommodate our bodies, slugged
on the driveway's concrete, stained
like the spots on hands you now
look down on to remember how
it felt to wield ratchets and grease guns...

You look upon your body's failure:

> deflated cartilage;
> the betrayal of symphyses;
> corroded articulations;
> diabetes; arthritis; bad blood...

but there is no Chilton manual, father,
to diagram a man's bodily virtue.

Studying The Jaw Of A Mechanic

Crescent wrench in hand,
knuckles bruised against bolts
that shot to clenched jaw,
but like you I ground
pain's metallic taste
between maxilla and mandible
until it softened to a pulp
easier to swallow...

I learned not to mention the wounds.

Father's Contemplation

In the familiar smells
of the tool shed

you thought
would some day

save you
from this,

below the mass
of head hung solitude,

the German Luger
felt strange

on your lap.

Dad, You Can Die In Peace Now

I woke up this morning,
forty-five years old,

the right measure
of dignity in my hands.

As I walked, I allowed
each step its measure.

I am sure my step was not
like anyone else's.

I am sure my hands
have changed forever.

A Rustic Vein

I saw my father till the Earth a spine,
the springtooth clawed through winter's reticence,
as She in turn gave poetry this line.

The discs made mince of clod to redefine
the rugged field. I braced the innocence
of watching father till the Earth a spine

as if my heart already knew to pine
the smell of dirt, the tractor's turbulence,
and Earth to turn for poetry this line

as straight the plow can furrow a design
to sow the seed of hunger's eloquence.
I saw my father till the Earth a spine

where rain, the sun, and prayers recombine
the molecules of Earth's magnificence
as She performed for poetry this line

that ground the vein of father's work so fine
a field that flowered wide as consequence,
I see my father till the Earth a spine
as She in turn gives poetry this line.

Fallen Fruit

Beneath the fig tree's bruja limbs,
where sunlight sifted shade from leaf
and fallen fruit was brown and succulent,
my grandfather was an immutable
mystical being, who in the span of a summer,
took the slow, deliberate, caustic tick of time
and swallowed it like a pill, every fiber
of his body ripe with truth.

Genealogy Of Men Who Hear Their Names In The Desert

Mine is an insignificant inheritance:
when I walk alone in the desert,
to hear my name...

      clear, neutral, unexaggerated...

as if an older me is calling

Ismael. Nothing else...

Like my father, *Antonio*,
my grandfather, *Hilarión*,
and all our forefathers,
who walked alone
the Mexican deserts:

      walking stick,
      sandals,
      peasant soul
      passed down like a modest curse...

And while other genealogies
branch from kings or tyrants,
the men in my family
hear their names in the desert.

III

SCREAMING IN THE BUGHOUSE

Morning Snow On The Prison Ground

for my friend, Bill

I   (prisoners)

I cannot think of a better day to write a letter:

the ground is a blank sheet,   the steps
of prisoners are words they never speak...

They just keep walking.

II   (angels)

I cannot believe this is everything:

over the Pinenuts Range,   the clouds
are scrolls of papyrus and I

with an eternity of love to write.

On Pogonip And Passing

—for Bill

I   (prisoners)

To write a last poem
would be to say
all my prayers are answered...

Yet I crave another Paiute winter,
for pogonip to ice the morning air:

a man must know how   to breathe these blades.

II   (angels)

I cannot close my eyes and think of you
nor swallow a promise without knowing
I haven't written in such a long time

even when I thought the doctor
would snow you, to make the pain all disappear,

and all your poems   fall like snow.

What Can Anyone Say About A Heavy Man Gone

—for g.c.

He loved
the one he killed,

then died
in prison,

without a word
in a million books of poems

to tell her
with a simple line

how alone he was in this world.

When Leaves Of Water Fall

I reach through my cell's barred window
for the warm midnight rain,
watch the drops explode on my palm—
my life line is long...

I wanted to sleep
but too fresh on my breath
the curse of startled-awake hands
grasping at your ghost.

It is embarrassing
but I have no deus ex machina
craned in to solve the unsolvable.

I toyed with the idea
of tying my hands behind my back
before I go to bed,

but then I would only
snap at you with my teeth...

I need my mouth to scream... not pray...

All my prayers end in doubt
but it was the voice I knew that night:

> *Please don't die.*
> *Stay for your children.*
> *Let me hear you*
> *yell at the dog*
> *through the kitchen window...*

Your lifeless eyes,
witnessed it all,
then stared at me
from the forensics photograph
on the defendant's table, accusing:

> *He tried to revive me*
> *but ran to the restroom*
> *to vomit.*

> *He fled through the kitchen door,*
> *with my last breath*
> *cupped in his hands,*
> *desperately trying to blow*
> *the embers back to life...*

Outside my cell,
soft as whispers,
leaves of water fall...

Everything I touch dissolves.

The Fig Tree's Hand of the Dead

I can't imagine dying
at my own hands,
holding that last breath—
because every time I hold my breath,
not to imagine,
but because I deplore
the thought of my hands and death—
I hold it only until
I start to breathe again.

And somehow
I can't tell the parole board
that breath
is how I pronounce remorse:
sorry that I am still breathing,
(breath)
that you have to put up with me,
(breath)
that I don't have the answers,
(breath)
sorry that my hell is wordless
and that heaven
does not speak to me,
that only the voices
to people I grew up listening
speak to me—
but they are all dead.

My mother says, *está bien,*
todo está bien—

but when she says
that everything is alright,
I have to caress
the top of my own head—
because her hands are dead.

And my father follows, *pues sí,*
así es la vida—
that that is life,
but I cannot wrap
my arms around his barrel chest—
because his barrel chest is dead.

So I pull the hug into myself
and bow my head
so she can reach me from the grave.

And never to vindicate,
I say to my grandfather,
I didn't know
what else to do but fight back—
but I fought back too hard,
too out of control,
too scared to remember
the voice of sacrifice (breath)
he taught me to summon:

that if a bird eats the fig,
then I eat the bird,
then the earth eats me,
a fig tree grows
from the seed in my belly,
and my soul is a tree in the sun,

that my soul then says,
thank you for the sacrifice,
and feeds the birds like an old man—
like my grandfather holding out his hands.
Then he says, *ten tú,*
dale de comer a los perros—
to practice by feeding the dogs
to feel the animals
live from my hands—
so that I may die
to be a tree like him...

Then I realize
I'd been holding my breath—
(breath)
because when I remember
the life I took,
(breath)
I don't feel like breathing—
because she is not breathing.

And I wonder
what kind of tree
grew from her belly—
and all the birds that feed from her hands.

Rousing Those Who Attend The Death & Dying Group

I
Mr. Fleming is lying still,
grey blanket snugged below the chin,
a half-there man waiting
for the great Surgeon
to remove the cancer
below his tongue,
or an angel to arrive
with news his application was accepted.

II
From the weight of his cross,
Mr. Lopez's head has collapsed again,
tired of piecing together
the world with mathematics and music,
swirling between theories of existence
and the counter tap/clap
of a Gypsy's boot and hands.

III
Grey hair easily distracted
by the unawares of his thoughts,
Mr. Day is lying wide wake, still wondering
why thousands and thousands of young men
had to give up their lives in a war.

IV

Knowing someday I may find myself
cradled in their aged pain,
I hold dear compassion for every caned step
taken from body-dented beds,
down white, sterile hallways,
into the group room
where trenches are exchanged for plastic chairs,
wood handled carbines
for styro-foam coffee cups,
where the old war cry has aged
from *kill them* to *dear God let me live.*

In A Group Of Failing Bodies

—for jim's death & dying group

The men in the group are dying.

No messiah walks
   on the surface of polished hallways
         to cure or kill.

Today we sit in a circle,
   wrapped in denial's conversation
         anticipate the talons of death

         to break water, extract us
         from below the calm
         surface of uncertainty.

I come close to knowing
I do not want this waiting to end.

But I am young,
   an anomaly in my health,
         a psych clerk for this group

         of men whose bodies fail.

I worry only to understand
   their consummate communion
         with breath and brevity.

If they ask me, I fear
   they will confuse me
      with the big bad boy

      flaring nostrils
      on an angry grey horse.

Postcard: Los Cholos

They look like Buddhist monks,
little bald heads and sun
browned skins, congregated in baggies,
throwing down signs against white t-shirts,
a new language born in their hands,
a new poetry spoken on the body,
sumi-ed on the brown bark sheets of their faces.

At 1721 Snyder Avenue

Prisoners with faded glares and cobbled skins,
gnarled hands, the took-away trembles,
brown nicotine-stained fingertips,
their never washed-out coffee cups,
empty, always begging for a shot—
I see them for freaks:

    carnival's formulary of the deformed,
    lacerated in the brightness of a father's cord,
    or kept too far from mother's hearth,
    step right up and see the show,
    the freaky-deaky dude with his big slick hand,
    slapping the back of a poker deck,
    the pinko-prince warrior tacked to the neck
    juggling crosses, bolts and a weiss macht 'tude,
    a border brother all baggy and brown
    with latent desires of joining the clowns,
    step up step up see the formaldehyde child,
    a wiz with a cig and bubble-eyed smile.

Yes, good people, step right up,
watch men in blue shirts and bluer yet hearts,
drink their coffee and crumble to dust.

A Stroll In The Park

If there were trees,
and fallen leaves,
girls in levi cutoffs,
circle dancing,
learning the ways
of women,
an old couple
locked in arm,
so familiar with
each other's step,
on a path
worn down,
a mother
in a sunny dress
talking to
her child
of the world,

and while
we're wishing,
a lake,
a bench for lovers,
and my bare feet
stretched out
on the grass
over which I see
the girls in cutoffs,
circle dancing,
this would not be prison.

Looking Out My Prison Cell At Freeworld Construction Workers Taking A Lunch Break

Two Mexican workers
sever from the group
to rest beneath
the alien shade of prison.

The old one opens up a book
while the young one bites
down on a burrito, paces
round, glances out at those
with English tongues—
makes it hard to swallow.

They say nothing, a tradition
from my own upbringing...

I think of my father
who thought the White
more clever because of war,
who taught me
to abandon my tongue—
something hard to swallow.

Listening To The Wind Ooo Beneath
My Prison's Metal Door

Through the bottom slit
of a closed, metal door,
the wind ooos

mean nothing,
empty as an
over-the-many-years

thought of giving up
day in and
day in,

like a prisoner's
harsh hands
full of exaggerations,

his fast
always-hands-moving
stories that take

nothing from
the listening man
to say I only know

between cement and metal door,
the wind strips the soul
with its nothing word.

Be White Black

—for Cole Johnson

He speaks well,
middle class collegiate tongue,
reads the rags
fashion brings to light:
the dress, the catch,
the coin-phrase etymology...

Today at a four-seat stainless table
he indoctrinates three white men
to the strategies of bridge.
I weave by,
intoxicated by the thought,
"How apropos: bridge ..."

Bridge black man,
befriend that white world,
find their Sun Tzo weakness,
dip your cup into their daughters' wells,
before back across the bridge
strapping your belt
into the crotch of black country
while your rasta/presbo seedlings
kick inside their pink-globed bellies,
they wonder where you go,
turn to wave, smile, and say,
I'll be white-black...

before you strike the match.

The Last Rites Of A Bastard

—Just keeled over. He was an asshole.

The deathwatch beetles click
stronger toward the last heart beats,
like the clicking of the dead
with their arid tongues
begging for the frenetic
trumpets of the Apocalypse...

       Chest compressions,
       mouth to mouth resuscitation,
       the dumb faces waiting
       for you to cough up pejoratives...

The paramedics tried
to dismiss
God's thirst
for the bitter water of your body.

An Ugly Man In Prison

Indian-style on a patch of grass,
you rock back and forth,
weaning off thorazine
with thick-as-oil coffee,
reciting Bob Dylan
to yourself for two hours.

Not once do you stop
to look beyond
the invisible friend you bless
with the words of a prophet,
not once do you mind
the ignorant scoff
of passers-by.

No one will remember
how you sat reciting Dylan
to a plastic mug of coffee,
and this afternoon,
after the medication
that keeps you from killing,
you will also forget.

Mr. Sutton's Moment of Clarity

Forget that his brain
has no language
for the accretion
of amyloid-beta peptides,
or the phosphate seduction
of tau proteins
to unravel
the neuronic
ancillary microtubules,
or that he is forever
the victim
of a bruja's binding spell
the doctors call Alzheimer's...

I want to know who
will witness
if some quiet
middle of the night,
he wakes up
to bellow the lung of litany,
an impetuous
unfolding of the tongue,
to recite Yosano Akiko
or Anaïs Nin,
or to unleash
his pale, atrophied body
from its diaper
to waltz
in the vacuous hall
of some fantasized castle,

his feet like the hooves
of an adept goat
as he dips and swoops,
then just as suddenly...

settles back down
to the derelict stare
of a stupid, old man
too deep gone
in a bruja's binding spell.

Tirado Dies In Prison Today

Nothing can stop Tirado
from dying today
in the prison hospital;
lymph nodes deflated
all dried out of miracles;
no elixir wrapped
in a brown paper sack;
only metastasized metaphors,
pathogenic parasites,
to bore through
the earth of his flesh
too scabbed by disease
to cultivate
save the seeds of cancer;
lungs that grapple
the trachea to scrape
the back of the tongue
for air or scraps
of love-sustaining poetry,
for what of life
without the song,
the vituperation of love...

I work as a porter
in the prison hospital
serving ice and tea
to the sick and dying,
but today I take
Tirado's plastic cup,
dab my fingertip

in salt I poured
into my pocket,
then around the rim
I trace
a shaman's blessed circle
that he may sip
through the spell
of an Aztec prayer:

> Tlazoltéotl, Eater of Filth,
> dance for Tirado
> in Your black huipil,
> then sweep his dust
> into Your blackness...
> because we both know...

Nothing can stop Tirado
from dying today.

The Old White Convict

The frugal movement seems cliché,
the steps are small, the body shakes,
and yet he gets around without
a cane nor common pleasantries,

he wheezes, coughs, expectorates,
then swears to God the summer heat
will melt his plastic teeth, then how
to chew the crap they serve at chow.

Emaciated as he looks,
the constant bitching never ends,
and so I wonder what it is
that keeps this geezer talking shit—

about the way that everyone
was put on earth to piss him off,
the raghead punks of Babylon,
the opium, the immigrants,

the gangbang slave mentality
with baggy pants that sag like clowns
to show their ass. He swears the whole
damned world has lost its fucking mind,

and he should know 'cause White is right,
he says as if to joke, but I
can hear the cross of bigotry
still burn below the Southern charm.

Jimmy Took Too Long To Die

Old bastard, rigid from the pain,
bleached-bone dentures
strained shallow breaths
down the sides of his neck
vile-veined and nerves so taut
every muscle in his twisted
body was a dry, leather knot.

Tired of his wheelchair, he stood
but Parkinson's legs were too bent
for nothing more than to stalk
like Nosferatus in the classic B-movie
who crept tipped-toe, hands
before him like a praying mantis
while the virgin slept...

But unlike the black & white vampire,
whose only perversion was
puncture wounds on the neck,
Jimmy took his victim's head clean off.

He never told them where he hid the head,
believing some glorious day he would get out
to claim his prize, to look again
upon her bleached-bone scream...

Had he not died in the prison hospital,
had the rest of us not seen him—
as he stammered around the yard
growling at everyone he hated to fuck off—

deform into an elongated cat's claw
that couldn't hold a cup
or change his own clothes,
one would believe even now
Jimmy's ghost does bad things.

Screaming In The Bughouse

"And when he had opened the fifth seal,
I saw under the altar the souls of them
who were slain...for the testimony
which they held."—Revelations 6:9

Now my arms are strapped to my chest,
a defeated child whose last defiant act
is to sit. My mouth is muzzled.
My feet, for wandering, have walked in
through the forest of my hairy legs.
They have climbed my ribs one step at a time,
jimmied their way up my throat,
and are stomping around in my brain.

     I can't stop the silence.

When the messiah comes, I want to be
the one who digs up the graves.
I want to see skeletons laughing,
party with those half decomposed.
I want to marry a skeleton girl,
love her every delicious bone.

I want to smith shoes for the pale horse,
befriend the beast with sugar cubes,
take it for a stride, gallop
like a carousel, round and round so fast,
the luminosity of atomic wisdom seeps
through the slits of my padded cell.

I hear a diaspora of screams in the hallway,
a religious recital, a prayer for the insane.
I'm in touch with my first mother,
a rogue singularity who broke her vow of silence.

Like a perfect child, I have all her characteristics:
roué, dissipated man, débauché, a rake,
raking up the leaves of stars,
dancing chucha huanga benshi waltz,
whipping my head like a whore.
I'm worthy of suffering on the wheel,
so spin.

       I can't stop the silence.

Diagonal thoughts denote evasive maneuvers,
parables, parenthetical puffs of smoke.
Designer drugs distract the mind
from its honest course of madness.
And the mad, the morally misplaced,
stuffed in this bughouse. The revival
of electric shock, abusive technicians
storm in six deep with needles:
Intramuscular vituperation, I dance
like a beatnik troubadour.

When the messiah comes, he will ask for directions.
I will lead him by hand to this bughouse,
where the blessed saints, pseudo-saviours,
state-sanctioned savages, dissect us like bugs,
screeching insects, as they...

They walk on the water of our tears.

The Visit

Through the prison gate
my old mother's skin
slung on a skeleton
hunched over her bloated stomach
stretched from too many pregnancies

she goes
through a list of names
before she gets
to mine
then smiles almost

before tears
run down her wrinkled cheek
whimpers against my neck
"Ay mijo,
when are you coming home?"

in my mind
I see the gavel
strike twice
once for each life sentence
I can feel my mother

sob her heart
faint
against my prison shirt
I kiss
her grey head

hold her tight
like she held me
when I
was just
a little boy

for six hours
we played cards and made
small talk about
the way things
used to be

how little Emma
found a man
she thinks will care
how papa
with his heavy arm

wrapped around Henry's neck
had to hold him
while mom called the cops
Henry lost his mind
in a cloud

sin semia and PCP
and even though we
tried to focus
on the cards we held
we'd catch a glimpse

of each other's eyes
tried to smile
like strangers
so our good-byes
wouldn't hurt too much

then some blur
with green pants and a badge
yelled like slow motion hate
"Time's up!"
and we forgot what

we were about to say
zombied our way
to the red line
where her world starts
mine ends

I realized I
was once umbilicalled
to her
my mother
my life blood

opened my arms
she melted
into my veins
my brain whirled
I wanted to go

as much
as she wanted
to take me
I assured her
everything would be all right

she gripped
a dizzy breath
exhaled hope
I would be out soon
squeezed me once more

I kissed her hair
tasted
a salty scalp
brought back a memory
of Oceanside Beach

where she held my hand
as I reached out
to touch
the green foam
she let go

I let go
as she walked
out the door
looked back to wave
a tall skinny cop

stopped from touching
her shoulder
let her leave
in her own
slow

way
in her own
pain
again
turned

around
to wave
good-bye
and pray,
"Soon mijo."

Mother, You Died While I Was In Prison

I think about how empty
the house will be without you.
The morning sound of things
coming back to life:

> fracas from the old, tin coffee pot
> brewing a dark roast to fill dad's thermos;
> the skillet stir of fried beans,
> roasted jalapeños and ground beef.
> Burritos wrapped in aluminum foil.

When the black metal lunch pale
is latched and he has left,
I will sift through the dark
to join you in the kitchen...

but you will not be there.

Meditation From A Cell

in all the universe, in all the worlds,
among every creature who ever loved,
the sand outside my cell is most enduring.

it says nothing of the poems i write to you,
the poems i tear, the blank page so flush of love...

this morning it waits with me for you to visit,
your hand to brush aside the sand
gathered in my eyes like a shoal of hungry souls.

The Muppets In Prison

I

The thug, the hood, the derelict,
the endemic cull of scofflaw;
but this prison also confines the old,
sent from the more robust
to this bastille's medical facility—
the senescent, their bodies curdled down
to dodder between despair and doom.

II

The prison's Coffee Shop is busy,
the eight prisoners, fortunate
for such an assignment, their hands
task to get the business running:

      the pizzas are thawed,
      the pull-from freezers restocked,
      the tickets run are marked,
      then filled by the pull room...

I man the window,
where every class of criminal,
every nature of human sin loom
like God's obscene, disfigured experiments
for their names to be called...

And the stupid, little song in my head begins to play.

III

Here come the muppets,
decrepit old prisoners, sporadic tufts
of dingy white hair, eyebrows thick
and askewed as burnt brier root,
bloodshot, droopy, little buttons
staring in through the Coffee Shop window.

How did these jalopies get here,
these sesame street rejects?

Wheelchair, cane, or the old-man-creep,
out of breath, out of their minds, the scent
of goodies dangling from nose hair.

There's one who stares so hard, I think he's dead,
but then begins to talk, face invigorates
with a sense of urgency, eyebrows, moustache,
hairy ears, all jittering about asynchronously.

Order filled, he pushes away
from the Coffee Shop window, as he might have seen
a comrade do, or he himself, back into
the cold ocean, back to the Unit before Pill Call,
back to dodder between despair and doom...

And as he does, I feel somewhat sad
and wish I had more conversation;
but I know this cold reality of consequence:

These muppets were evil and did bad things.

ABOUT THE AUTHOR

Ismael García Santillanes now lives back in the small, agricultural town, Mecca, California, where he spent many of his formative years. This is where he learned to look upon land seemingly lifeless with wonderment. Yet life is a matter of degrees, like seed catching in the split bark of dried up mesquite, or sweat dripped onto the skin of that seed. This is the xeric mind of the desert, where not much is needed to fulfill the promise of breath and brevity. And so, he writes always from the heart desert sand carved.

COLOPHON

Designed and produced by Bob Blesse at the Black Rock Press, University of Nevada, Reno. The typeface is Quadraat, designed by Fred Smeijers, a Dutch type designer. Printed and bound by BookMobile, Minneapolis, MN.